SCENES OF THE AUSABLE RIVER VALLEY

PHOTOGRAPHS BY PETER CISZEWSKI **POST CARDS** HAND-TINTED BY MARLA MERANTE

AUSABLE PRESS

HCR 1, Box 46
Keene NY 12942

ISBN 0-9672668-0-7

Ausable Press publishes poetry
and the Bark Eater series of books on the Adirondacks.

This is a Bark Eater book.

CAMP INTERIOR
Photograph © Peter Ciszewski
Hand-tinted by Marla Merante

PLACE
STAMP
HERE

AUSABLE PRESS, HCR 1 Box 46, Keene NY 12942

PURE
MAPLE
SYRUP
FOR SALE

SUGARING AT RIVERMEDE FARM
KEENE VALLEY, NY
Photograph © Peter Ciszewski
Hand-tinted by Marla Merante

PLACE
STAMP
HERE

AUSABLE PRESS, HCR 1 Box 46, Keene NY 12942

THE BARGE
AUSABLE LAKES
Photograph © Peter Ciszewski
Hand-tinted by Marla Merante

PLACE
STAMP
HERE

AUSABLE PRESS, HCR 1 Box 46, Keene NY 12942

CANOE
UPPER AUSABLE LAKE
Photograph © Peter Ciszewski
Hand-tinted by Marla Merante

PLACE
STAMP
HERE

AUSABLE PRESS, HCR 1 Box 46, Keene NY 12942

THE UPPER AUSABLE RIVER
Photograph © Peter Ciszewski
Hand-tinted by Marla Merante

PLACE
STAMP
HERE

AUSABLE PRESS, HCR 1 Box 46, Keene NY 12942

THE AUSABLE RIVER
Photograph © Peter Ciszewski
Hand-tinted by Marla Merante

PLACE
STAMP
HERE

AUSABLE PRESS, HCR 1 Box 46, Keene NY 12942

REPEATING
RIFLES
SKI-TOW
PARKING
PAINT
TYDOL
DAIRYLEA
ICE CREAM

GEORGE JAQUES ANTIQUES
KEENE VALLEY, NY
Photograph © Peter Ciszewski
Hand-tinted by Marla Merante

PLACE
STAMP
HERE

AUSABLE PRESS, HCR 1 Box 46, Keene NY 12942

THE AUSABLE CLUB
ST. HUBERT'S, NY

Hand-tinted by Marla Merante

PLACE
STAMP
HERE

AUSABLE PRESS, HCR 1 Box 46, Keene NY 12942

FIVE BIRCHES
Photograph © Peter Ciszewski
Hand-tinted by Marla Merante

PLACE
STAMP
HERE

AUSABLE PRESS, HCR 1 Box 46, Keene NY 12942

KEENE CENTRAL SCHOOL

KEENE CENTRAL SCHOOL, 1999
Photograph © Peter Ciszewski
Hand-tinted by Marla Merante

PLACE
STAMP
HERE

AUSABLE PRESS, HCR 1 Box 46, Keene NY 12942

KEENE VALLEY
E DEPT.

VOLUNTEER FIRE DEPARTMENT, 1998
KEENE VALLEY, NY

Hand-tinted by Marla Merante

PLACE
STAMP
HERE

AUSABLE PRESS, HCR 1 Box 46, Keene NY 12942

HITCHHIKER
Photograph © Peter Ciszewski
Hand-tinted by Marla Merante

PLACE
STAMP
HERE

AUSABLE PRESS, HCR 1 Box 46, Keene NY 12942

RAINBOW FALLS
Photograph © Peter Ciszewski
Hand-tinted by Marla Merante

PLACE
STAMP
HERE

AUSABLE PRESS, HCR 1 Box 46, Keene NY 12942

LAN
OF NEW YORK
RTMENT
OF
ENV NMENTAL CONSERVATION
PRIMITIVE
For the primates from N.Y.C.
AREA
Rockerfellow's Zoo.

BOUNDARY LINE
Photograph © Peter Ciszewski
Hand-tinted by Marla Merante

PLACE
STAMP
HERE

AUSABLE PRESS, HCR 1 Box 46, Keene NY 12942

SNOW CANOEING
Photograph © Peter Ciszewski
Hand-tinted by Marla Merante

PLACE
STAMP
HERE

AUSABLE PRESS, HCR 1 Box 46, Keene NY 12942

LEAN-TO IN SNOW
Photograph © Peter Ciszewski
Hand-tinted by Marla Merante

PLACE
STAMP
HERE

AUSABLE PRESS, HCR 1 Box 46, Keene NY 12942

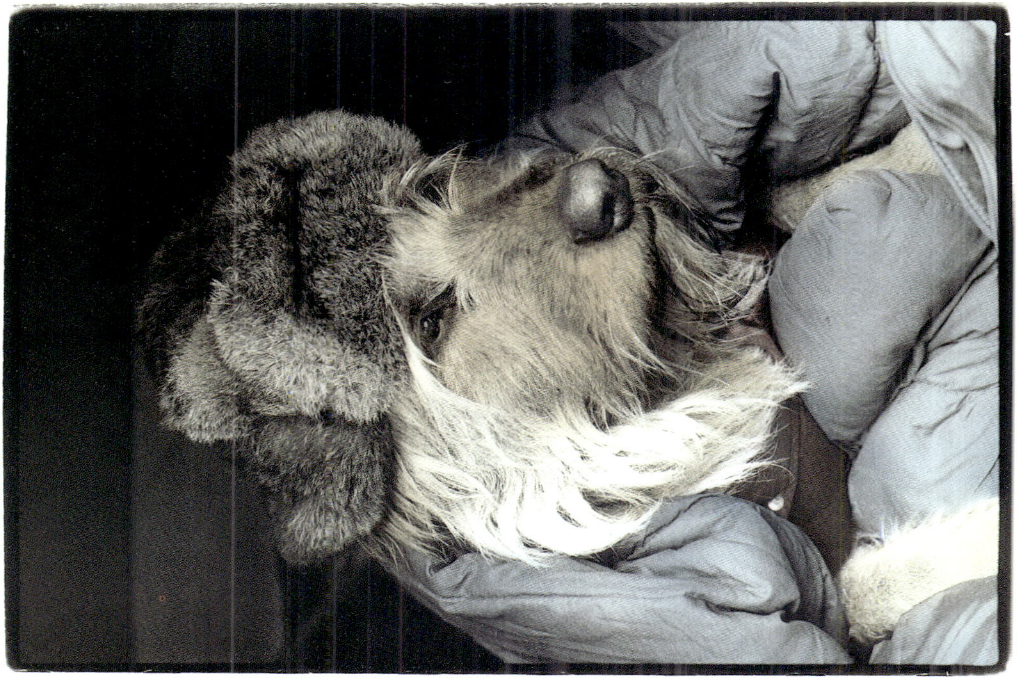

BAILEY
Photograph © Peter Ciszewski
Hand-tinted by Marla Merante

PLACE
STAMP
HERE

AUSABLE PRESS, HCR 1 Box 46, Keene NY 12942

MARLA AND "BEAR"
AMERICAN BASHKIR CURLY STALLION
RUNNING HORSE FARM
Photograph © Peter Ciszewski
Hand-tinted by Marla Merante

PLACE
STAMP
HERE

AUSABLE PRESS, HCR 1 Box 46, Keene NY 12942

ADIRONDACK BED & BREAKFAST
Photograph © Peter Ciszewski
Hand-tinted by Marla Merante

PLACE
STAMP
HERE

AUSABLE PRESS, HCR 1 Box 46, Keene NY 12942

WINTER RAYS, HIGH PEAKS
Photograph © Peter Ciszewski
Hand-tinted by Marla Merante

PLACE
STAMP
HERE

AUSABLE PRESS, HCR 1 Box 46, Keene NY 12942

Pete Ciszewski, photographer,
and Marla Merante, painter,
live in the Adirondacks with their friends,
a border collie to watch over running horses,
and the mountains that they call home.

SCENES OF THE AUSABLE RIVER VALLEY

Twenty Tear-Out Post Cards

AUSABLE
PRESS

HCR 1, Box 46
Keene NY 12942

ISBN 0-9672668-0-7

51000

EAN

9 780967 266800

$10.00